BEGINNING SOCIAL STUDIES

FOLLETT

NORTH AMERICA

ATLANTIC

N
W   E
S

Columbus lands here
on October 12, 1492

Bahamas

San Salvador

Cuba

Hispaniola

Columbus sails for home
January 16, 1493

SOUTH
AMERICA

Clara
Ingram
Judson

OCEAN

EUROPE

Genoa

Portugal

SPAIN

Palos

Azores

Columbus returns to Palos
March 15, 1493

Columbus sails from Palos
August 3, 1492

AFRICA

Canary Islands

Christopher
Columbus

Text Illustrations by Polly Jackson

Title Page design by Stan Williamson

FOLLETT Publishing Company · Chicago · New York

Library of Congress Catalog Card Number: 60-9126

SIXTH PRINTING

TLA 1201

The path up the big rock began at the end of the street. It went to the top of the big rock.

When Christopher Columbus was a little boy, he climbed up the rock by himself. He sat down and looked around.

He saw houses below him. He saw all of the city of Genoa.

He saw ships and the wide blue sea. The ships had yellow sails and orange sails. Christopher liked ships.

He saw men working with the sails.
The sailors looked very small from the
top of the rock.

A ship moved away. The wind blew
against its orange sails. That made the
ship move faster.

The wind blew Christopher's red hair.
He liked the wind. He liked the sea.

I am going to be a sailor,
Christopher thought. I want to go to sea.
I want to sail far away.

Christopher knew it would not be
easy for him to go to sea. His father
was not a sailor. He was a weaver.
He made cloth. And in Genoa, 500 years
ago, a boy learned his father's work.

Christopher did not go to school.
He helped his father with his work.
He was learning to be a weaver.

7

Christopher had good times, too.
His father liked to fish. Some days he
took his two sons fishing in his boat.

They rowed by the big ships.
Sometimes sailors on the big ships waved
at the two boys.

After they passed the ships,
Christopher's father put up a sail.
Sailing was faster than rowing. Soon
they were far out to sea.

When Christopher was older, he could sail the little boat himself.

"I like to sail a boat," he said. "I would like to learn to be a sailor."

"You must learn to be a weaver," his father said.

Christopher learned to wash wool. He learned to spin wool into thread.

But he still wanted to be a sailor.

One day he met a ship's captain.

"Please, sir," he said, "will you take me for a ship's boy?"

The captain looked at Christopher. The boy was tall. He looked strong.

"We sail early in the morning," the captain said. "The work is hard."

Christopher ran home.

"I like the sea and the ships, Father," he said. "May I go?"

His father was sad. But he said, "You may go, my boy."

At last Christopher was going to sea.

Before the sun came up the next morning, the ship sailed away.

Every day Christopher worked hard. He washed dishes. He washed the deck. He did everything the captain told him to do.

Every day he watched the sailors work with the sails. He watched the sky. He learned the names of stars and where to find them in the sky.

I am learning to be a sailor, he thought. I must remember everything.

The captain saw that Christopher did everything he was told. He saw that the boy wanted to learn. He took Christopher to sea with him again and again.

As years went by, Christopher learned to climb up high and work the sails like a man. He learned what to do in a storm.

A ship was like home to him.

Young Columbus sailed the sea to the south, to the east, and to the north. He saw many cities.

Then he went on a ship that sailed into the great ocean. Now I am a real sailor, he thought.

After that Columbus sailed on the ocean many times. He sailed south and north on the ocean. But sailors did not sail very far west on the ocean.

Men were afraid to sail very far from land. There was enough danger on the ocean not very far from land.

Once Columbus was in great danger.
His ship went down to the bottom of
the ocean. Many sailors died.

But Columbus could swim. He saw
some wood in the water. He held on to
it and swam to land.

The land Columbus came to was called
Portugal. His brother lived in Portugal.

14

Columbus' brother lived in the biggest city in Portugal. He worked at making maps and selling them.

Columbus worked with his brother. He learned to read and write and to make maps. He learned to read maps other men made.

He read books and talked with men who knew many things. Columbus liked this. He wished he could know about the whole world.

Columbus married a lady of Portugal. Her name was Felipa. Her father had been a friend of the king.

Felipa had a room full of her father's fine books and maps. Columbus looked at the maps. He read the books.

He read about a place called the Indies, or the Far East. These were other names for countries like China, Japan, and India. The Far East had gold, jewels, and spices that people wanted.

Columbus talked to other men about
the Indies. The sailors of Portugal were
great seamen. For a long time they had
been trying to reach the Far East by
sailing south around Africa.

They wanted to find a way by water.
It took a long time and cost more to go by
land than by water. Men were often killed
by bandits when they went by land to the
Far East. The sailors of Portugal looked
for a better way to get to the Indies
and the gold and jewels and spices.

Columbus sailed many times from
Portugal. He sailed south and north.

He listened to sailors talk. He thought
about what they said.

After a time Columbus thought there
was a better way to get to the Indies
than by sailing around Africa.

Since the earth was round, if a ship
kept on sailing west, it would get
to the East.

18

Columbus needed ships and sailors
to try out his plan. He did not have the
money to build ships and to pay sailors.

So he went to the king of Portugal.
He asked the king to pay for the ships and
men he needed to sail west to the Indies.

"Sir," Columbus said, "I will find
new lands and great riches for you."

But the king would not help Columbus.
The king did not believe in his plan.

The king of Portugal laughed at
Columbus and his plan. He went away sadly.

After a time, Columbus left Portugal.
There was nothing to stay for. The king
laughed at him, and Felipa had died.

Columbus took his little son and went
to Spain. From the ship they went to a
monastery.

The good fathers at the monastery
kept the little boy. They would feed him
and give him a place to sleep. They would
teach him to read and write.

The fathers helped Columbus too.
They helped him to meet a man who said
he would take him to the queen of Spain.

The queen wanted to make Spain a
great and rich country. Maybe she would
give Columbus the ships and men he needed.

But the king and queen of Spain were
fighting a war. They were with the army,
far away. It was a long time before
Columbus saw the queen.

When at last Columbus did see the queen, he told her about his plan to sail west to the Indies. The queen asked her wise men what to do.

The wise men thought and talked for a long time. Then they told the queen not to give Columbus the ships and men.

The plan was not a good one, the wise men said. The ocean was much bigger than Columbus thought. The ships would never be able to come back to Spain.

But Columbus knew he could do what
he said. And the queen seemed to believe
in him and his plan.

"We have no money for ships now,"
she said. "Come back when the war is over."

Columbus waited for years. Then, as
he was about to go to another country to
ask for help, the queen sent for him.
The war was over.

"I will pay for your ships, Columbus,"
said the queen. "I will sell my jewels
if I have to."

At last! Columbus could hardly believe
it. But he hurried to get ships and men.

On the third day of August, 1492,
three ships were ready. Columbus stood
on the deck of the biggest ship.

He looked proud and handsome.
His red hair was white now. He was forty
years old.

Columbus gave the word, and soon the
ships were moving. People on shore watched
as the ships sailed down the wide river
to the ocean.

For weeks the ships sailed on and on,
where no one had sailed before. The men
had not seen land for a long time.

The weather was good. The wind
filled the sails and made the ships go
fast. But as more weeks passed, and they
saw no land, the sailors said:

"We should be in the Indies by now."

They sailed on. But still they saw
nothing but water and sea birds.

Columbus stood on deck looking to the
west. He was still sure he would reach
the Indies. He tried to cheer his men by
telling them of the riches they would have.

But the sailors were afraid.

They said: "We have seen no land for
many weeks. But we keep on sailing west!"

"Every day Spain is farther away!"

"We should make Columbus turn back
or throw him in the ocean!"

On the ninth day of October the men talked to Columbus.

"We must turn around and go home!" they said.

Columbus said, "If we do not see land in three days, we will turn back."

The next day sailors saw land birds flying near the ship.

In the water they saw branches of trees with green leaves.

Land must be near!

Early in the morning of October 12, 1492, the lookout shouted, "Land! Land!"

Everyone ran to see if it was true. They saw land.

Columbus was full of joy. He put on his best clothes and went ashore.

He knelt down and thanked God for bringing them safely to land. Then he planted the flag of Spain.

People with brown skins came to see
Columbus. He called them Indians.
He thought he had come to the Indies.

He did not know he had come to a
new land. It was a land that people to
the east did not even know about. It
was a New World.

Now, each year, October 12 is a
holiday. On that day people honor
Christopher Columbus, the brave sailor
who discovered America.

CHRISTOPHER COLUMBUS

Reading Level: Level Three. *Christopher Columbus* has a total vocabulary of 368 words. It has been tested in upper second grade classes, where it was read with ease.

Uses of This Book: An excellent introduction to history and geography concepts. An interesting biography which will make Columbus Day more meaningful to children in the primary grades. Good for older slow readers.

Word List

5 the
path
up
big(ger)(gest)
rock
began
at
end
of
street
it(s)
went
to
top
when
Christopher('s)
Columbus(')
was
a **6**
little
boy(s)
he
climb(ed)
by
himself
sat
down
and

looked(ing)
around
saw
houses
below
him
all
city
Genoa
ship(s)('s)
wide
blue
sea
had **7**
yellow
sail(s)
orange
like(d)
men
work(ing)(ed)
with
sailor(s)
very
from
move(d)
away
wind
blew

against
that
made **8**
fast(er)
red
hair
I
am
go(ing)
be
thought
want(ed)
far
knew
would
not
easy
for
his
father('s)
weaver
cloth
in
500
year(s) **9**
ago
learn(ed)(ing)
did

school
help(ed)
good
time(s)
too
fish(ing)(ed)
some
day(s)
took **10**
two
son(s)
boat
they
rowed(ing)
sometimes
waved
after
passed
put
sail(ing)(ed)
than
soon
were
out
old(er)
could
said
you

must
wash(ed)
wool
spin
into
thread
but
still
one
met
captain
please
sir
will
take
me
tall
strong
we
early
morning
is
hard
ran
home
may
sad(ly)
my

11 last
before
sun
came
next
every
dishes
deck
everything
told
do
watch(ed)
sky
name(s)
stars
where
find
them

12 remember
again
as
high
man
what
storm

13 young
south
east
north
many
cities
then
on
great
ocean
now
real
west
afraid
land(s)
there
enough
danger

14 once

bottom
died
swim
wood
held
swam
called
Portugal
brother
lived

15 making
maps
sell(ing)
read
write
make
other
books
talk(ed)
who
things
this
wished
know
about
whole
world

16 married
lady
her
Felipa
been
friend
king
room
full
fine
place
Indies
or
these
countries
China
Japan

India
gold
jewels
spices
people

17 seamen
long
try(ing)
reach
Africa
way
water
cost
more
often
killed
bandits
better
get

18 listened
since
earth
round
if
kept

19 needed
plan
money
build
pay
so
ask(ed)
new
rich(es)
believe

20 laughed
left
nothing
stay
monastery
feed
give
place

sleep
teach

21 meet
queen
country
maybe
fighting
war
army

22 told
wise
much
never
able
come
back

23 seemed
no
over
waited
another
sent
have
hardly
hurried

24 third
August
three
ready
stood
proud
handsome
white
forty
gave
word
moving
shore
river

25 weeks
seen
weather
filled

should
birds

26 tried
cheer
telling
keep
farther
turn
throw

27 ninth
October
see
flying
near
branches
trees
green
leaves

28 lookout
shouted
everyone
true
joy
best
clothes
ashore
knelt
thanked
God
bringing
safely
planted
flag
Spain

29 brown
skins
called
Indians
even
holiday
honor
brave
discovered
America

Follett Beginning Social Studies Books

Follett Beginning Social Studies books contain accurate, up-to-date information about our world—its history and geography, its people and their ways of life. These books are designed to provide pleasure in reading and to give children the information they need to enrich their lives and their school work.

Follett Beginning Social Studies books are written for the primary grades. They are completely illustrated. They cover a wide range of subjects, adding interest to the familiar and shedding light on the unfamiliar.

Christopher Columbus

Understandings Developed in This Book

It was not easy for the son of a weaver to go to sea.

Boys were supposed to learn their fathers' work. Christopher Columbus started learning to be a weaver. But he wanted to be a sailor so much that his father let him go to sea.

Christopher Columbus did not go to school.

Children then did not all go to school. Christopher Columbus was a grown man before he learned to read and write. He learned about maps from his brother. He learned about the world by reading books and studying maps.

What sea voyages were like then.

Voyages were long. Ships did not have engines then. They could only go by being rowed, or by being pushed by the wind blowing on the sails. They could not go very fast. Sailing was dangerous. Men were afraid to sail far from land. There was enough danger close to land.

Columbus had a hard time getting people to believe in his plan.

Columbus believed in his plan for getting to the Indies by sailing west. But the plan was new and strange. It was hard to make poeple see that it might work.

Columbus had to get money from a king or queen.

His plan would cost so much that only a king or queen would have enough money to help him.

It took courage to go far out on the ocean.

Nobody had ever sailed where Christopher Columbus wanted to go. Many people were sure the ships would never come back. The sailors were afraid. But Columbus was sure they would reach the Indies if they kept on.

Why Columbus wanted to find a new route to the Indies.

People wanted the gold, jewels, and spices of the Indies. It was dangerous to go there by land because there were bandits along the way. It was a long costly trip by land. People needed to find a way to get there by water.

Christopher Columbus made an important discovery.

Columbus did not find the way to the Indies that he was looking for. But he did find a land that nobody knew about. It was so important that people called it the New World. His voyage opened the way for people to explore and settle in the New World.